Spiritual Sisters

Edited by

Ven. Thubten Chodron

Other books by Thubten Chodron:
Open Heart, Clear Mind
What Color Is Your Mind?
Taming the Monkey Mind
Glimpse of Reality, with Dr. Alexander Berzin

Front cover: Kuan Yin (Avalokiteshvara, the Buddha of Compassion)
and Our Lady of Guadalupe.

Additional copies available from:
Dana Promotion Pte. Ltd.
c/o Blk 31 Dover Road
#05-117
Singapore 130031

Printed in Singapore by
Internal Printers
4035 Ang Mo Kio Ind. Park 1 #01-51
Avenue 10
Singapore 569642

ISBN 981-00-7653-3

Contents

Contents

Introduction:

Religious Diversity and Religious Harmony

If someone had told me when I was twenty years old that I would become a Buddhist nun, I would have told them they were crazy. Not only could I not imagine being celibate or curbing my attachment to pleasures of the senses, but also I thought religion was harmful. Having studied history in university, I learned that almost every generation in Europe had seen a war over religion. Millions of people have been killed in the name of religion throughout history, and I thought, "What use is religion if it causes harm?" Over the years, I have come to understand that the problem is not religion *per se*, but the disturbing attitudes in the minds of human beings that make them misunderstand the meaning of whatever religion they follow. The holy beings--Buddha, Jesus, Mohammed, Krishna, Moses, and others--would be distressed by what beings with limited understanding do in their name.

One of the chief misunderstandings that we ignorant beings are prone to is "the sports team mentality" towards religion. We identify with one sports team or religion and then, juxtaposing it with another, think that ours has to be the best. We cheer for our religion, and try to convert others to it so that it will have more members. We think that the more people be-

1

lieve in it, the truer it must be. We put down other religions in an attempt to prove to ourselves that ours is supreme. This is a useless pursuit, one that leads to disharmony and even violence in society, and is contrary to the real intent of all religions.

This attitude misunderstands the purpose of religion, and confuses sincere religious practice with religious institutions. While we can measure the number of people who call themselves Jews, Muslims, Buddhists, Hindus, or Christians, we cannot measure the depth of understanding and experience of any of those people. Being religious is more than attaching a certain label to ourselves; it is transforming our minds and hearts so that we become better people. Being truly religious occurs in our hearts--no one else can see this with their eyes. Religious institutions, however, can be seen and measured. We must ask ourselves, "What is my purpose? Is it to be religious or to promote a religious institution?" Religions have their source in mystical experience; religious institutions are the creations of imperfect human beings. They are designed to facilitate religious practice, but whether religious institutions are successful in doing this depends on the human beings who are their members. One can be deeply religious and not belong to any religious institution. Similarly, one can promote a religious institution and not have any feeling in one's heart for the lofty principles that religion advocates.

All religions are for the purpose of human happiness. They all teach ethics and compassion and stress harmony among people. Philosophically there are differences, and while recognizing those, we can still appreciate the similarities. His Holiness the Dalai Lama once said that he believes the real religion is compassion. We experience the compassion of others from infancy throughout our lives. Without the kindness and efforts of others, it would be impossible for us to sustain our lives alone. Compassion in ourselves enables us to live harmoniously with others and eventually to experience a peaceful death. People from all faiths agree with this. We experience compassion naturally simply by being a human being. However, our knowledge of doctrines such as creation or karma is learned later on.

Sometimes people ask, "Wouldn't it be better if there were only one religion in the world and everyone believed in it? Then there would be no fighting among the various faiths." While we may be initially attracted to this idea, from a Buddhist viewpoint the multiplicity of religions is necessary and desirable. First, it would be impossible to make each and every human being believe in the same philosophical or religious tenets. People clearly have different ways of thinking and different tendencies, and there is no way to make all of them hold the same beliefs. Second, it would not be beneficial for only one religious system to exist in our world. Because people have different tendencies and attitudes, a variety of religions is necessary to ensure that each person can find one that serves him or her best. Different systems of thought and practice inspire different people. As long as a person endeavors to live ethically and harmoniously, which religion he or she follows--if any--is irrelevant.

Are They All One?

We sometimes have difficulty accommodating the fact that there are so many different religions, and find comfort in thinking that they are all essentially the same--they are like different paths up the same mountain or like surveying many valleys from the same mountain top. Many people believe that the founders of each religion had the same mystical experience of reality. The words describing an experience are never the same as that experience. They are simply approximations, human attempts to convey in words what is by nature inexpressible and inconceivable. Thus many people postulate that the founders of the various religions selected words from their respective cultures to describe mystical experiences which were essentially identical. Later generations, however, focused more on the words than on the experience, and that is the source of philosophical differences among religions. Some people speculate that the Trinity in Christianity is another formulation of the three kayas in Buddhism. Others say that God the creator is the equivalent of karma, or that God the ultimate is the equivalent of Dharma--the true path and true cessation of suffering.

While it is possible that these theories are correct, it is not possible for us ordinary beings to determine so. Philosophically there seem to be clear differences in approach. For example, Christianity speaks of an everlasting soul while Buddhism talks of the lack of a permanent, singular, independent self or soul. By practicing according to the philosophy of one system will one generate the same mystical experience as practicing according to another system? Only a person who has followed both systems to their ends, gaining direct realizations of both paths, could discern this through his or her own experience. Only then could one ascertain for sure whether the two religions originated from and pointed to the same experience of reality. For those of us who have not gained direct realizations of our own religion, let alone of other faiths, it is presumptuous to say that they lead to either the same or to different goals. We must simply remain content to say, "It's possible that all religions point to the same mystical reality, but I don't know." Most importantly, we must practice according to our faith and transform our hearts and minds into compassion and wisdom.

Fortunately, for religious harmony and interreligious dialogue to occur, it is not necessary to conceptually juggle the different beliefs to make them the same. We can accept the variations in philosophy and even rejoice in them. Hearing views different from our own strengthens our ability to investigate; it challenges us to have a deeper understanding of the philosophy we study. It also calls us to investigate what is true, rather than to be waylaid by simply repeating the words of the religious texts without understanding or experiencing their deeper meaning.

The Value Of Interreligous Dialogue

What, then, is the value of interreligious dialogue? How should it be conducted? The purpose is to benefit people, not to debate and arise victorious. When we approach dialogue with an open mind, respect and willingness to learn, we benefit others and are benefited in return. However, if we or the other party lack this attitude, then it is better not to discuss religion. For communication to occur, there has to be a sincere wish not simply to speak but especially to listen. If this is missing, it is best to excuse ourselves from the conversation. Were it to continue, the discussion would degenerate into an issue of power, not spirituality, with one party trying to dominate or convert the other. Genuine interreligious dialogue occurs in an atmosphere of mutual respect and genuine interest. It is a sharing of spirituality that inspires all parties. Someone once observed, "When philosophers and theologians meet, they argue. When spiritual practitioners and mystics meet, they smile."

Through my experience of talking with people of other faiths, I see many things we can learn about both their similarities and differences. In terms of the similarities, first, it becomes evident that the chief obstacles to any form of spiritual practice are materialism and attachment to pleasures of the five senses, praise and reputation. All spiritual people agree about this. We can only cultivate ourselves spiritually to the extent we understand the disadvantages of being distracted by and attached to external pleasures. The mind that craves more and better--be it more or better material possessions, fame, approval, or pleasure from the senses--has limited energy to direct toward the cultivation of ethics, love, compassion or wisdom. All spiritual traditions emphasize letting go of our worldly attitudes. Second, there are similarities in life style. In the dialogue that follows, two nuns--one Catholic, the other Buddhist--discuss the challenges of living without financial security, remaining celibate, and living in community. Although our philosophical beliefs differ, we understand each other's life style and practice at the heart level.

Practitioners of various faiths also share similar experiences, for example, riding the ups and downs that occur in spiritual practice. For example, years ago Sister Kathleen England came to visit our Buddhist monastery in France. She had been a nun for over fifty years and had worked in the Vatican. At first, we had some "conflict" because she wanted to learn about our practice but we wanted her to tell us about hers! Finally, after we each had a chance to listen to the other, I asked her, "How have you handled the crises that arise when practicing? How do you deal with those 'dark hours of the heart' when you are filled with self-criticism or doubt?" She gave invaluable advice: "When we go into crisis, it signifies not that we are backsliding in our practice, but that we are ready to grow. Our previous understanding, which worked for a while, is no longer sufficient. We need to go deeper, and we are ready to do so. That is why the crisis occurs. It is an invaluable time for growth, because as we work our way through it, we come to understandings that we were not able to have before." What I learned from Sister Kathleen has enabled me to remain a Buddhist nun all these years.

Another experience people from differing religions may share is that of preserving their religious practice and culture when they live as a minority in a foreign land. Because thousands of Tibetans have been living in exile in India and elsewhere since 1959, they have become intrigued by the Jewish experience of preserving their religion in **Diaspora**. In recent years mutually beneficial interreligious dialogue has occurred between Jews and Tibetan Buddhists. The Tibetans have learned about the value of family rituals and community activities in preserving their unique religion and culture as a minority group in another country, while the Jews have had a new look at meditation and mysticism and were encouraged to spread the teachings in their own tradition on these topics.

People from various religions can learn a great deal from each other's practices. For example, His Holiness the Dalai Lama often praises the social work that Christians undertake in society: the schools, orphanages, homeless shelters and hospitals they set up and work in, and the aid they give to refugees and to the poor. He encourages Buddhists to learn from the example of their Christian brothers and sisters and to engage in projects for the benefit of society at large. On the other hand, he says, Christians can learn meditation techniques from Buddhists. In Buddhism, the methods to calm and focus the mind are described very clearly. These can be practiced by people of any faith and applied to their own religious system. They can also be practiced by people who have no particular faith and simply seek to quiet their minds and eliminate stress. Thus dialogue with people from other religions can show us practical ways to better live according to the principles of our own religion.

Interreligious dialogue helps us to become more open-minded. It also sharpens our abilities to investigate and to examine ourselves and our beliefs. Spiritual people want their limited views to be expanded; they seek to have their ignorance removed; they want their capacity for understanding and acceptance to be stretched. Interreligious dialogue presents this possibility. However, what happens if we are not prepared for this and the dialogue instead causes defensiveness or confusion about our own practice to arise? Seen from the proper perspective, this too presents an opportunity for growth. For example, when we talk with a person from another religion and find ourselves becoming defensive, we must examine our minds. Have we fallen into the trap of subtly competing with the other person to prove one religion right and the other wrong ? If so, we need to let go of our "sports team mentality" and remind ourselves of the real purpose of our conversation. No one else can make us feel inferior: this attitude arises from our own competing mind. When we cease this, then there are no winners or losers.

Are we defensive because we worry about the other person liking and approving of us? Has our religion become part of our ego-identity so that if our religion is criticized, we feel misunderstood and rebuked? We have to question our need for external validation of our beliefs. Why do we need other people to believe the same thing we do in order to feel secure in our beliefs? We may have forgotten that people have different aptitudes and temperaments and will therefore see things differently. If we have checked the foundations for our spiritual beliefs and have confidence in them, there is no need to become defensive because others disagree with them.

But what if we have not examined our beliefs deeply? What if the other person asks a question that we do not know the answer to and we become confused about what to believe? What do we do if interreligous dialogue causes our ignorance to become evident or doubts to arise in our minds? Uncomfortable though this may feel initially, this in fact could be valuable for our practice. When we do not know the answer to a question or cannot explain it clearly, it indicates that we need to ask our teachers and spiritual friends for more information. In addition, we need to spend more time reflecting on what we already know in order to understand it properly. When we listen to teachings, we sometimes think we correctly understand the entire topic. In fact, we may have understood the words, but because the meaning is multi-layered, we need time to explore it in depth. It is unrealistic to expect ourselves or others to be able to "know all the answers." Doubt or confusion can be helpful stimulants pulling us out of our complacency. We do not need to be afraid of these things. We simply need to deepen our practice, researching the answers to questions and reflecting on their meaning.

Making Peace With Our Past

The audience for this book is diverse. Some people who read it will be Buddhist, some Christian, some of other religions, others of no religion. Similarly, some will be Americans, some Singaporeans, some from other countries. Therefore, it could be helpful to look at issues that might arise for different people when they consider interreligious dialogue.

In recent years, many Westerners have become interested in Buddhism. Some of them have negative feelings toward the religion they learned as children. This could happen for several reasons: a religious teacher or leader misunderstood them or unfairly disciplined them; religion was forced upon them by parents or teachers; they disagreed with the sexism or other prejudices displayed in the religious institutions; they found so-called "religious people" to be hypocritical, elitist, judgmental or closed-minded. If we encounter another religion that better meets our needs, it is all too tempting to vent previous frustration and see everything from the religion we grew up in as negative. However, it is extremely important to make peace with our past, not to reject it. If we stereotype an entire body of practitioners and judge them, we have become closed-minded and prejudiced. Such resentment and bias obstruct our practicing our new faith. When we have this type of "negative loyalty" to something from our past, we often reenact the very thing we disapprove of. Although we may think we are free from the influence of something because we have rejected it, in fact that thing may have a great hold on our mind because so much of our energy is tied up in disliking it.

Thus, having a negative attitude toward the religion we learned as a child blocks our spiritual development. It is also unrealistic, for despite the things we do not like or disagree

with, we did learn many good things from our childhood religion. For example, it instilled in us many ethical principles that
enable us to live in harmony with others. It taught us the value
of love and compassion. It encouraged us to believe that
something was more important than our self-centeredness. It
taught us that there is another kind of happiness besides the
short-term happiness we receive from pleasures of the senses.
All these things laid a foundation in us for further spiritual
training, and thus in part helped us to connect with the spiritual beliefs of our new religion. When we think deeply, we
realize that we received benefit from our childhood religion,
even though it may not be the one we choose to practice as
adults. We must avoid painting anything as all good or all bad.
Thus, it can be helpful for Westerners who have become Buddhists to reflect upon both the strong points and the weak-
nesses of their religious up-bringing so they can reach some
emotional and philosophical resolution regarding them. Such a
process could also be helpful for Asians who grew up as nomi-
nal Buddhists and later became Christians.

Coming Out Of The Closet

Some educated Singaporean Buddhists are shy to tell their
colleagues at work that they are Buddhist. In Singapore, some
people think that if one is Christian, then one is more Western
and modern. Therefore, some Buddhists think that if others
know they are Buddhist, others will look down upon them as
"old-fashioned." Also, because some Christians in Singapore
are evangelical, the Buddhists fear meeting with unpleasant
pressure to attend church or read Christian literature. Indeed,
aggressive religious propagation is unfortunate and damaging
to harmony in society. However, that need not make us embar-
rassed about our religious beliefs or upset with people who are
unskillful.

Similarly, some Westerners are shy about telling their colleagues or family that they are Buddhist. Unlike the Singaporean Buddhists, these Westerners do not fear being considered old-fashioned. Rather, they are concerned that others will think they are different or strange. Although Western culture seemingly promotes individuality, there is tremendous pressure to conform and to do, think, or believe like others. Westerners fear that they will not be accepted or approved of if they do not share the same perspectives as the group.

It is difficult to practice our religion if we lack confidence in it or in ourselves. Embarrassment over telling others we follow a particular faith could come from a couple of sources: first, we are not sure about what we believe and why; or second, we are attached to our reputation and fear losing friends. When we have not spent time thinking about our beliefs or if we do think about them but still have major doubts, then inter-religious dialogue could appear threatening to us. We harbor fears: "Maybe I will not know the answer to a question," "Maybe I will inadvertently misrepresent Buddhism," "Maybe I will respond incorrectly and the other person will refute it. What will I believe then?" When asked a question that we cannot answer with assuredness, we can simply reply that we do not know but will research it. There is no need to feel humiliated or insecure because every Dharma teaching is not clear in our minds. After all, we are not yet Buddhas!

We must look closely at our attachment to reputation and to being liked by others. Will others really ostracize us if we have different views? Why is others' approval so important to us? If others have different views, does that mean ours are wrong? Is the only basis for friendship having the same religion? Many of these fears are projections of our minds. If we are kind people and try to communicate effectively with them, they surely will respond positively to us no matter what our religion. If, due to their closed-mindedness, others remain aloof, there is nothing we can do. It is not necessary that eve-

ryone likes us or approves of us. We do not need external
validation to be sure of our spiritual path or of ourselves. We
need internal confidence that arises from contemplating the
truths of the Buddha's teachings and applying them to our
lives.

Equanimity and self-confidence are the antidotes to embarrassment or insecurity about our beliefs. We cultivate equanimity by remembering that reputation is simply others'
opinions--thoughts in their minds that can change very quickly
and are not reliable. In addition, people will always have a variety of opinions, some agreeing with ours and others not. It is
legitimate for diverse beliefs to exist. Human contact and
warmth come through sharing the experience of being human
beings, not through holding the same philosophies. Self-
confidence is developed by remembering that we--and others--
have the Buddha potential. We may not be totally wise or
compassionate now, but we can become that way. This awareness of our internal goodness and potential is a more stable
basis for self-confidence and self-esteem than other people's
opinions of us. If we are aware of this, we will not be dis-
turbed by what others think of us, but will continue to relate to
them with a kind heart.

It is possible that the opposite happens, that is, that we become critical and impatient with people who have worldly values or who are not Buddhist. We must look at where such
intolerance comes from within us. Why do we insist that everyone be like us? Could insecurity be fueling our intolerance?
To be kind-hearted , it is not necessary that people call themselves Buddhist. We must avoid becoming attached to labels,
for this breeds the "sports team mentality." Relating to people
with an open heart and respecting them is what the Buddha
prescribed. We are neglecting the meaning of the teachings if
we fall prey to a self-righteous, judgmental attitude. Since each
person has the Buddha nature or potential--or to put it in

Christian words, since each person is the creation and image of God--he or she is worthy of our respect.

About This Book

This book contains several examples of interreligious dialogue. "Spiritual Sisters: A Benedictine and a Buddhist Nun in Dialogue" is a talk given by Sister Donald Corcoran and Ven. Thubten Chodron in September 1991, at the chapel of Anabel Taylor Hall, Cornell University, Ithaca, New York. It was cosponsored by the Center for Religion, Ethics and Social Policy at Cornell University and the St. Francis Spiritual Renewal Center. Ven. Chodron went to the Transfiguration Monastery, Sister Donald's community in Windsor earlier that day. The two sisters prayed together and then spent many hours in discussion ranging from philosophy to the practical aspects of living in community. The audience at Cornell was diverse-- Asians and Americans, Buddhists, Christians and agnostics. Many of them commented afterwards that the example of two women from different spiritual traditions discussing their own and the other's religious traditions with respect and interest was very inspiring. It demonstrated that meaningful dialogue which enhances each person's understanding of his or her own spiritual tradition could occur. The audio tape of their talk at Cornell is available from Snow Lion Publications.

"The Value of a Monastic Way of Life" is a talk by His Holiness the Dalai Lama to a group of Christian and Buddhist monks, and lay associates at the Monastery of Christ the King, Cockfoster, London. It belongs to the Benedictine Congregation of Monte Oliveto. The talk was given on September 17, 1994, at the conclusion of the John Main seminar, during which H.H. the Dalai Lama had for the first time commented extensively on the Christian gospels. Earlier that morning H.H. the Dalai Lama meditated with the Benedictine monks. The seminar is recorded in the video series "The Good Heart" from Medio Media in London.

"Love Unbounded" tells of the three-day visit of Sister Candasiri and Sister Medhanandi, two Theravadin Buddhist nuns from Amaravati Monastery in England, to the Sisters of the Love of God, one of the few Anglican contemplative Orders, at Fairacres, The Convent of the Incarnation, on the outskirts of Oxford.

I would like to thank Sister Donald Corcoran for the many rewarding discussions we shared together and for editing her section of the manuscript. I also appreciate His Holiness the Dalai Lama and Sister Candasiri for giving their permission to reprint their articles. "The Value of a Monastic Way of Life" was reprinted by permission of *Shambhala Sun* from the May 1995 issue. "Love Unbounded" was reprinted from the *Forest Sangha Newsletter* and Amaravati Publications retains the copyright. Many thanks to Cindy Felis for transcribing the talk; to Michael Ruffra for his valuable editing suggestions and for proof-reading the book; to Dharma Friendship Foundation for supporting me while I worked on this book; to Wong Kam Chuen for designing the cover; to Dana Promotion Pte. Ltd. for arranging for its publication; and to the many kind sponsors who made it possible. All errors and omissions are my own. My sincere wish is that *Spiritual Sisters* will encourage spiritual practitioners to learn from each other, thus strengthening the practice of all spiritual traditions, reducing prejudice and enhancing harmony among people.

Thubten Chodron
Seattle WA, USA
June 13, 1995

Spiritual Sisters: A Benedictine And A Buddhist Nun In Dialogue

by Sister Donald Corcoran and Venerable Thubten Chodron

Life As A Benedictine Nun

Sister Donald:

We have great fortune to be here together, to learn from each other and to share with each other. This evening I would like to speak about four topics: the monastic archetype, my particular tradition, how I came to be a Benedictine nun, and spiritual formation.

The Monastic Archetype

Monasticism is a worldwide phenomenon: we find Buddhist monks and nuns, Hindu ascetics, the Taoist hermits of China, the Sufi brotherhoods, and Christian monastic life. Thus, it's accurate to say that monastic life existed prior to the Gospel. For whatever reasons, there is an instinct in the human heart which some persons have chosen to live out in a deliberate and continual way for their entire life; they have chosen a life of total consecration to spiritual practice. In a New York Times book review of Thomas Merton's poems a number of years ago, the reviewer commented that a remarkable thing about Merton was that he made an extreme life option *seem* reasonable. That was a wonderful comment about monastic life! It is an extreme life option: the normal way is the life of the householder. The way of the monastic is the exception, and yet I think that there is a monastic dimension to every human heart-- that sense of the absolute, that sense of a preoccupation with the ultimate and what it means. This has been lived out and concretized historically in several of the major religious traditions of humankind. So, Chodron and I are here this evening to speak to you and share with you about our own experience in our traditions as women monastics and what monastic life means.

The Benedictine Tradition

I am a Roman Catholic Benedictine and love my tradition very much. In fact, I think any good Buddhist would tell me that I am far too attached, but maybe a little ebullience like that creates some success. Many years ago a sister from another order told me, "Maybe we should just finish with having so many Orders in the Church and have just one group called the

American Sisters." I said, "That's fine. As long as everyone wants to be Benedictine, that's fine!"

Founded in 529, the Benedictine order is the oldest monastic order of the West. St. Benedict is the patron of Europe and is called the father of Western monasticism. Two and one-half centuries of monastic life and experience happened before him and he is, to some extent, the conduit through which the earlier traditions--the spirituality of the desert fathers, John Cassian, Evagrius, and so on--were channeled through southern France, Gaul. The source that Benedict primarily used, "The Rule of the Master," is a distillation of much of that two and one-half centuries of monastic experience and tradition. Benedict added a pure Gospel rendering and provided a form of monastic life that was the *via media*, a way of moderation between extremes. It was a livable form of monastic life that was created just at the time the Roman Empire was crumbling. Thus Benedict's monastic lifestyle and his monasteries became a backbone of Western civilization, and the Benedictine monks saved much of classical culture--manuscripts and so forth. The sixth to the twelfth centuries are called by historians the Benedictine Centuries.

Benedict represents a kind of mainline monastic life. Both men and women have existed in Benedictine monastic life from the beginning because St. Benedict had a twin sister named St. Scholastica, and she had a convent nearby his monastery. Even when the Benedictines finally were sent to England by Pope St. Gregory the Great--St. Augustine--Benedictine nuns were established very early on the Isle of Thanet off of England. In that way the male and female branches of the Order have existed right from the beginning in the Benedictine tradition. In fact, this is true also of the older religious Orders in the Catholic Church: the Franciscans and Dominicans both have male and female branches, although as far as I know, there are no female Jesuits--yet.

17

The Benedictine way of life is a balanced life of prayer, work, and study. Benedict had the genius to provide a balanced daily rhythm of certain hours for prayer in common--the Divine Office or Liturgical Prayer--times for private prayer, times for study--a practice called *lectio divina*, a spiritual reading of the sacred text--and time for work. The Benedictine motto is *ora et labora*--prayer and work--although some people say it's prayer and work, work, work! This balanced life is a key to the success of the Benedictine tradition. It has lasted for fifteen centuries because of a common sense, and because of an emphasis on Gospel values. Benedict had a great sensitivity for the old and the young, the infirm, the pilgrim. For example, an entire chapter of the Rule deals with hospitality and the reception of guests. One way the Benedictine motto has been described is that it's the love of learning and the desire of God. The Benedictines have a wonderful sense of culture and a great tradition of scholarship.

Women have been very important in the Benedictine tradition. Women like St. Gertrude and Hildegarde of Bingen, who has been rediscovered in the last five or ten years, have always been important in the Benedictine tradition. Earlier today when Chodron and I met, we discussed transmission and lineage, and although we in the West don't have the master/disciple type of lineage that Buddhism has, we do have a kind of subtle transmission in the monasteries, a spirit that carries over from generation to generation. For example, an abbey of Benedictine nuns in England has a unique style of prayer which they trace back four centuries to Augustine Baker, the great spiritual writer. The nuns in this monastery pass this tradition on from one person to another. Monasteries are great reservoirs of spiritual power and spiritual knowledge in the tradition; they are a priceless resource.

In early Buddhism, monastics wandered from place to place in groups and were stable only during the monsoon sea-son. Chodron told me she is continuing this tradition of wandering, even if it be by airplane! Meanwhile, the Benedictines are the only order in the Roman Church that has a vow of stability. That doesn't mean that we have a chain and ball and have to literally be in one place. Rather, at the time Benedict wrote the rule in the sixth century, there were a lot of free lance monks wandering around. Some of them were not very reputable, and these were called the gyrovagues, or those who traveled around. Benedict tried to reform this by creating a stable monastic community. However, throughout the history of the Benedictines, there have been many who have wandered or who have been pilgrims. Even I have been on the road a lot for someone who has a vow of stability! The essential thing, of course, is stability in the community and its way of life.

My Vocation And Experience As A Nun

I trace my vocation back to when I was in the eighth grade and my maternal grandmother unexpectedly died of a heart attack. I was suddenly confronted with the question, "What is the purpose of human existence? What is it all about?" I remember very clearly thinking, "Either God exists and everything makes sense, or God does not exist and nothing makes sense." I reflected that if God exists, then it makes sense to live entirely in accordance with that fact. Although I was not going to a Catholic school and did not know any nuns, in a sense that was the beginning of my vocation because I concluded, "Yes, God exists and I am going to live entirely in terms of that." Although I was a normal child who went to Sunday Mass, but not daily Mass, I really didn't have much of a spirituality before this sudden confrontation with death brought me to question the purpose of human existence.

19

A few years later, in high school, I began to perceive a distinct call toward religious life and Benedictine life in particular. It was at this time that I felt the rising of desire for prayer and contact with that divine reality. In 1959, I entered an active Benedictine Community in Minnesota that engaged in teaching, nursing, and social work.

I have been a Benedictine for more than thirty years now, and I think it is a great grace and a wonderful experience. I have no regrets at all; it's been a wonderful journey. At the beginning of my monastic life in Minnesota, I taught as well as lived a monastic life. As time went on I felt that I wanted to concentrate on my spiritual practice; I felt a call to contemplative life and didn't know how I would live this out. For six years I taught high school, and then came to the east coast to study at Fordham. Increasingly I began to sense that living a contemplative life was the right thing to do, but before that was actualized I taught at St. Louis University for three years. I knew two sisters who were in Syracuse and intended to start the foundation from scratch in the Diocese of Syracuse, and I asked my community in Minnesota for permission to join them. But before doing that I decided that I should visit first, and so in 1978 drove from St. Louis to New York City, with a stop in Syracuse. On the Feast of the Transfiguration, I drove from Syracuse to New York City and on the way was almost out of gas. I pulled into the little town of Windsor, and as I drove down the main street, said to myself, "It would be nice to live in a small town like this." The sisters had no idea where in the Diocese of Syracuse they were going to locate. Six months later I got a letter from Sister Jean-Marie saying that they had bought property in the southern tier of New York about fifteen miles east of Binghamton. I had a funny feeling that I remembered what town that was, and sure enough, it was Windsor. I believe the hand of God has been clearly guiding me along the way, specifically to Windsor.

After teaching graduate school in St. Louis for three years, I moved to Windsor to work with the other sisters to start a community from scratch, which is quite a challenge. Our aim is to return to a classical Benedictine lifestyle, very close to the earth, with great solitude, simplicity, and silence. Hospitality is a very important part of our life, so we have two guest houses. We are five nuns, and we hope to grow, although not into a huge community. We have a young sister now who is a very talented icon painter.

One privilege that I've had within the Order is that for eight years I was on a committee of both Benedictines and Trappists--monks and nuns--who were commissioned by the Vatican to begin dialogue with Buddhist and Hindu monks and nuns. In the mid-seventies, the Vatican Secretariat dialogued with the other major religions of the world and said that monastics should take a leading role in this because monasticism is a worldwide phenomenon. For eight years I had the privilege of being on a committee that began the dialogue with Hindu and Buddhist monks and nuns in the United States, and we sponsored visits of some of the Tibetan monks to American monasteries. In 1980, I was sent as a representative to the Third Asian Monastic Conference in Kandy, Sri Lanka, which was a meeting of Christian monastics in Asia. Our focus for that meeting was on poverty and simplicity of life, and also the question of dialogue with other traditions.

Spiritual Formation

What is spirituality all about? To me, spirituality or the spiritual life comes down to one word--transformation. The path is about transformation, the passage from our old self to the new self, the path from ignorance to enlightenment, the path from selfishness to greater charity. There are many ways that this can be talked about: Hinduism talks about the *ahamkara*, the superficial self, and the *atman,* the deep self that one attains through spiritual practice. Merton talked about the transition or the passage from the false self to our true identity in God. The Sufi tradition discusses the necessity of the disintegration of the old self, *fana,* and *ba'qa,* the reintegration in a deeper, spiritual self. I am not saying that all of these are identical, but they are certainly analogous, even homologous. Tibetan Buddhism talks about the vajra self, and it is interesting that Theresa of Avila in *The Interior Castle* describes going inward to the center of her soul through steps and phases of spiritual practice. She said, "I came to the center of my soul, where I saw my soul blazing up like a diamond." The symbol of the diamond, the vajra, is a universal or archetypal symbol of spiritual transformation. The diamond is luminous--light shines through it--and yet it's indestructible. It is the result of transformation through intense pressure and intense heat. All true spiritual transformation, I believe, is a result of spiritually intense pressure and intense heat. In the *Book of Revelation,* chapter 22, there's a vision of the heavenly Jerusalem which is the consummation of the cosmos or the consummation of our individual spiritual journey. The writer of the *Book of Revelation* describes a mandala: "I saw the vision of the city, a twelve-gated city and in the center was the throne with the Lamb on it, the Father/Son, and a river of life flowing in four directions, the Holy Spirit." This is the Christian trinitarian interpretation. As the author of the *Book of Revelations* describes it, the waters were crystal or diamond-like. That light of the grace of God, the divine, the ultimate that transforms us is that crystal light, that diamond-like luminosity that shines through us. We chose to name the monastery at Windsor Monastery of the Transfiguration, because we believe that monastics are called to be transformed themselves in order to transform the cosmos; to transform not only ourselves, but the entire world; to let that light, that luminosity, radiate out from us to all of creation.

Another way that the Tibetan Buddhists talk about enlightenment is the intermarriage of wisdom and compassion. I've thought about this, and may be stretching your meaning of it a little bit, but I think that in each human being there is a tendency towards love and a tendency towards knowledge. Those basic virtues, those instincts in us, must be transformed in order to complete love and knowledge. Our love is like the anima that must become animus, and our knowledge is the animus which must become anima. That is, our knowledge must become wisdom by becoming loving, and our loving must become wise in order to be transformed. I believe that we can identify that process leading to the intermarriage of wisdom and compassion in all the great paths of holiness.

I haven't said much about women and women's experience, but we'll get to that in the discussion after our presentations. Chodron and I certainly had some interesting discussions about it today at the monastery! I believe scholars have found that perhaps the first evidence of any sort of monastic life was with the women who were Jains in India. Perhaps the first monastic life in history that we know of was a women's form of monastic life.

Life As A Buddhist Nun

Venerable Chodron:

I would like to start by briefly describing the history of Buddhist monasticism and then relate my own experience as a nun. Some people might find it interesting to know how somebody who grew up in America ended up with a hairdo like this! Finally, I'll discuss the challenges of Buddhism coming to the West.

Buddhist Monasticism

Buddhist monasticism began about 2,500 years ago in ancient India, during the lifetime of Shakyamuni Buddha. The monks and nuns--sangha as they are called--were wandering mendicants as this was the life style of religious practitioners at that time. Hindu ascetics still follow this tradition today. The sangha depended on the public for their support, going from home to home to receive offerings of food from householders. In turn, the sangha taught the Dharma--the Buddha's teachings--to the lay people. During the heavy monsoon rains the sangha would stay in simple dwellings instead of wandering from place to place as they did during the rest of the year. After the time of the Buddha, these communities grew more stable and eventually became permanent residences for monks or nuns.

The lineage of nuns' ordination exists from the time of the Buddha. The first nun was his aunt, who raised him after his mother's death. Although the nuns were subordinate to the monks in terms of institutional power, their spiritual capabilities were recognized. *The Therigatha* contains teachings from some of the nuns who were highly realized, direct disciples of the Buddha.

From India, Buddhism spread to Sri Lanka in the third century B.C.E. Southeast Asia also became Buddhist: Buddhist, as did present-day Indonesia, Pakistan, and Afghanistan. Buddhism spread to Central Asia and to China from there, as well as from India by sea. From China, Buddhism spread to Korea and Japan. In the seventh century C.E., Buddhism entered Tibet from both China and Nepal. Now it is coming to the West.

There are three levels of nuns' ordination: bhikshuni, siksamana and sramanerika. To receive full ordination, that is to become a bhikshuni, one needs to be ordained by both ten bhikshunis and ten bhikshus (fully ordained monks). Giving the lower ordinations doesn't require as many people. As a result, the situation of ordained women differs in various Buddhist countries due to the level of ordination available to them there.

The daughter of the great Buddhist King, Asoka, brought the bhikshuni ordination from India to Sri Lanka. From Sri Lanka it went to China and then afterwards to Korea. Although the full ordination for men (bhikshu) spread to Tibet, that for women did not because it was difficult for so many bhikshunis to travel over the Himalayas. Thus only the first level of ordination, the sramanerika, spread to Tibet. In later years, the bhikshuni ordination died out in Sri Lanka due to political repression of Buddhism. Currently, Sri Lankan women can take the ten sramanerika precepts. In Thailand, Cambodia and Burma, the men can become bhikshus, yet the female ordained practitioners are in a kind of limbo situation. While they are not really lay people because they have taken celibacy vows, they have not taken the ten precepts of the sramanerika (novice).

The lineage of full ordination, bhikshuni, is flourishing in Chinese and Korean Buddhism, and there has been a resurgence of interest in it among women of all the Buddhist traditions. Some of us have gone to Taiwan, Hong Kong, Korea or the USA to take the bhikshuni ordination because it isn't presently available in our own Buddhist tradition, and people have begun to discuss how to make it available in these traditions in the future. Introducing the bhikshuni ordination has to be done slowly because it involves major shifts of thinking in the traditions that haven't had the full ordination of women for many centuries.

The external form of Buddhism has changed and adapted to different cultures as it went from one country to another. However, the essence of Buddha's teachings hasn't changed.

For example, at the time of the Buddha, the robes were saffron in color. In China, only the emperor was allowed to wear that color, so the robes became a more subdued gray or black. Also, according to Chinese culture, exposing one's skin was not polite, so the Chinese robes now have sleeves. The Tibetans didn't have saffron-colored dye, so the color of the robes became a dark saffron, or maroon.

Another example of how the form of Buddhism adapted to different cultures regards how the sangha--the monastic community--receives the material requisites for life. In ancient India, the monastics humbly went from door to door to collect alms from the laity who considered it an honor to help religious people in their practice. The Buddha set up the relationship of sangha and laity as one of mutual help. The people who wanted to dedicate their lives fully to spiritual practice wouldn't spend time working, farming, cooking and doing business. They could have more time to study and meditate by receiving support from the people who preferred to live and work in the world. By concentrating on their practice and developing their qualities, the monastics would then be able to teach the Dharma and be an inspirational example to others. Thus the Buddha set up a system of mutual help with one party giving more materially, the other more spiritually. Each person could choose how to help the society.

The tradition of collecting alms continued as Buddhism spread to Sri Lanka and Southeast Asia, and the vow not to handle money was strictly kept there. But in Tibet, this wasn't practical. The monasteries were outside the towns, and to walk in the freezing weather every day to go on almsround wasn't practical. Thus, the Tibetans started bringing food to the monasteries, or they would offer money or land so the sangha could get their own food. In China, the Ch'an (Zen) monasteries were far from towns, so the monastics worked the land to grow their food. Thus the economic situation of the sangha differs from country to country, depending on the culture and specific circumstances in each place.

My Experience

I didn't grow up as a Buddhist; my up-bringing was in a Judeo-Christian environment. My family was Jewish, although not very religious, and the community I grew up in was Christian. As a child, I asked many questions, "Why am I here? What's the meaning of life?" Because I grew up during the Vietnam war, I wondered, "Why do some people kill others if they all want to live in peace?" I grew up during the race riots, so I wondered, "Why do people discriminate against others on the basis of their skin color? What does it mean to be a human being? Why can't we live together?" I didn't find answers forthcoming in the community I grew up in. In fact, often my questions were discouraged. I was told, "Just go out with your friends, have a good time and don't think so much." But that didn't satisfy me.

After graduating from UCLA in 1971, I traveled in Europe, North Africa and went overland to India and Nepal to learn more about the human experience. I then came back to Los Angeles and worked in the L.A. City Schools, teaching in an innovative school. One summer I saw a flyer in a book store about a three-week meditation course taught by two Tibetan monks, Lama Yeshe and Zopa Rinpoche. It was summer vacation, so I went. I wasn't really expecting anything--in fact, I didn't know what to expect--and maybe that's why the experience was very powerful for me. The course was set up so that we listened to teachings and meditated on them afterwards. We examined them logically as well as applied them to our own lives.

As I did this, pieces began to fall into place and I began to get little twinklings of answers to the questions that had been

27

with me since childhood. In addition, Buddhism provided many ways of working with situations that happen in our daily life: it gave techniques to transform destructive emotions like jealousy, clinging attachment or anger. When I practiced these, they affected my life in a very positive way. As time went on, the wish grew to become a nun in order to have more time and a more conducive life style for practice. This was my own individual choice, and it's not the one everyone should make. Many people meet Buddhism, practice it and don't get ordained. But when I did some close introspection, it was clear how deep-rooted my selfishness, anger and clinging were. I needed some clear discipline to break the old mental, verbal, and physical habits. Becoming a nun would give me the framework in which to do this transformation, and this in turn, could positively influence others.

In 1977, I took sramanerika vows in Dharmsala, India, and spent many years studying and practicing in India and Nepal. As Buddhism began to spread to the West, my teachers were asked to open centers in other countries, and they sent their older students to help set these up. So, I spent nearly two years living in Italy, and three years in France, going back to India in between. In 1986, I went to Taiwan to take the bhikshuni ordination, which was a very powerful and inspiring event in my life. Later my teacher asked me to go to Hong Kong and then Singapore to teach. And now, I'm in the midst of an eight-month teaching tour of the States and Canada. So I have been a wandering, homeless nun, just like those at the time of the Buddha; only now we travel by plane!

What was it that attracted me to Buddhism? There were several things. In the first course, Zopa Rinpoche said, "You don't have to believe anything I say. Think about it, check it logically and through your own experience before believing it." I thought, "Whew, that's a relief," and listened because there was no pressure to believe anything. In Buddhism it's very im-

28

portant to reflect on the meaning of the teachings, to examine them deeply. This gives rise to faith, but not in the sense of blind faith. Faith, in Buddhism, is confidence that comes from learning and understanding. This inquisitive approach fits in with my upbringing. I like discussion and debate, and appreciate the freedom to ask questions and challenge what is said. This is possible with Buddhism.

Buddhism is open to scientific investigation. His Holiness the Dalai Lama has participated in several conferences with scientists and is eager to learn about research. He has even given permission for scientists to run EEGs and other tests on meditators in order to explain from a scientific viewpoint what is happening during meditation. His Holiness has also said that if science can definitely prove something, we Buddhists must accept it, even if it contradicts what is said in the scriptures. I find the openness to scientific investigation refreshing.

Buddhism and science are similar in explaining the universe in terms of cause and effect. That is, things don't happen without cause or by accident. Everything happens due to causes. The present is a result of what has existed in the past, and we are now creating the causes for what will exist in the future. This isn't predetermination by any means; rather, there is a link between the past and the future and things don't exist as isolated events in space. While science deals with cause and effect in the physical domain, Buddhism explores how it functions in a mental one.

When applied to our human existence, cause and effect becomes a discussion of rebirth. Our consciousness doesn't exist without causes. It's a continuation of the conscious experience that we had prior to this birth. Similarly, our consciousness will continue after our death. In other words, our body is like a hotel that we temporarily live in, and death is similar to checking out of one room and into another. Just as we don't cling to hotel rooms because we know we're just there temporarily, we don't need to fearfully cling to this body as a permanent personal identity.

I found this discussion of rebirth very stimulating. Although I wasn't convinced about it at first, as I examined it logically and listened to stories of people who remembered their previous lives, it began to make more sense to me. Although I don't remember my previous lives, when I look at my own experience, the theories of rebirth and karma can explain it. For example, Buddhism accepts the influence that genetics and the environment have upon us. However, the influence of genetics and the environment alone doesn't suffice to explain my experience. Why did I become a Buddhist? Why did it strike such a deep chord in me that I decided to become a nun? Genetically, there are no Buddhists in my family tree. Environmentally, there weren't any in my childhood. I grew up in a middle class community in southern California and had very little exposure to Buddhism except in social studies class. Yet somehow when I came in contact with the Buddha's teaching, something clicked, and it did so strongly that I wanted to dedicate my life to the path of spiritual transformation. It seems that one possible explanation would be that there had been some familiarity with Buddhism in previous lives. There was some imprint, some connection with Buddhism that lay dormant in my youth. When I was twenty, if someone had told me I would be a Buddhist nun, I would have told them they were completely crazy. I had no intention to be religious or to be celibate at that age! When I later met Buddhist teachers, this interest came out, much to my own surprise.

Another thing that sparked my interest in Buddhism was its psychological dimension, especially the discussion about the disadvantages of self-centeredness and the specific techniques to develop love and compassion. As a child, I heard people say, "Love thy neighbor as thyself." But I grew up during the Vietnam war and didn't see a lot of love in society. Nor did I understand how we were supposed to love everybody because there seemed to be a lot of obnoxious people around! Buddhism explains a step-by-step method how to diminish anger, how to see others as lovable, how to let go of the fear of opening ourselves so that we could genuinely care for others. I was very attracted to these qualities and to the systematic way to train our mind along these lines.

I was also attracted to Buddhism because for over 2,500 years people have practiced the teachings--the Dharma--and attained the results the Buddha described. In this day of the American spiritual supermarket, when there are so many self-declared teachers of a myriad of spiritual paths, Buddhism is one that was tried and true for centuries. The fact that the teachings have been preserved, practiced and passed down purely is important.

The practice of meditation also appealed to me. Buddhism describes specific techniques for quieting the mind and for getting to know ourselves. In Buddhism, there isn't a split between intellect and feeling or between intellect and intuition. They can help each other. In other words, if we use our mind astutely, if we employ reason to examine our experience, an inner transformation of our feelings, of our mental state, will come about. Experience and intellect can be combined instead of seen as a dichotomy as we so often see them in the West. This enables them to complement each other and produce internal growth, rather than conflict.

Bringing Buddhism To The West

As a first generation Buddhist nun in the West, I face many challenges and my "upbringing" as a Buddhist nun has been different from that of Asian nuns, who have long-standing Buddhist traditions and institutions in their cultures. They take ordination, enter the monastery, and pick up what it means to be a nun by osmosis, through living in the community. They receive instruction in their own language and have the support and approval of the society around them.

The situation is very different for Western nuns. Western society doesn't understand what people like me are doing. "Why do you shave your head? Why do you wear funny clothes? Why are you celibate? Why do you sit on the floor with your legs crossed and eyes closed?" There aren't monasteries in the West for us to move into where we can get a good Buddhist education. Although many Asian teachers have established Dharma centers in the West, they are primarily designed to suit the needs of lay Buddhists who work and have families. So many nuns go to India to receive teachings and to practice, thus encountering the bureaucratic, financial and health-related difficulties associated with living there.

Financial support for Western nuns has not been readily forth-coming. People in the West usually think that we're already taken care of by a large umbrella organization like the Church, so they don't think to make donation for our sustenance. Another difficulty for the nuns is lack of role models. For those following Chinese Buddhism, this is less of a problem because the Chinese nuns are active and educated. However, for those of us in the Theravada or Tibetan traditions, there are few living role models, although there were many great female practitioners throughout history. In my instance, I am a Western woman, while the majority of role models in the tradition are Tibetan men.

These difficulties have led me to look deep inside and gradually to accept the situation, instead of wasting time wishing it were different. Buddhism contains methods for transforming adverse circumstances into the path, and in this way I've discovered advantages to being a first generation Western nun. First, in Asia, it's easy to rely on the Buddhist environment all around to give one the energy to practice. In the West, the environment is often the opposite; it tries to convince us that material possessions, sex, beauty, prestige, but not religion, bring happiness. To survive in this environment, we have to look deeply within ourselves to find inspiration and spiritual energy. This forces us to understand the purpose and methods of religious practice, because it's either sink or swim. I've had to accept that what I experience--the opportunities as well as the obstacles--is the result of my previously created actions, or karma. Knowing that what I think, say and do now will create the causes for future experiences, I must think carefully and be mindful in the present.

Bringing Buddhism to the West is a challenge, because we're trying to bring the essence of a religion or a spiritual path from one culture into another. Buddhism in Asia is mixed with Asian culture, and sometimes it's difficult to figure out what is Buddhism and what is culture. When I first became a nun, I wasn't aware of the difference between culture and essence, between form and meaning. In my mind, it was all Buddhism and I tried to adopt it the best I could. Thus, I tried to act like the Tibetan nuns, who are meek and quiet. They would never think of speaking to a group like this or of writing a book or of challenging what has been said. Tibet is a very patriarchal society. Although in the family and in business men and women are more or less equal, in Tibet's religious and political institutions they aren't. The Tibetan nuns' shyness could be a sign of their humility, which is a quality to be cultivated on the path, or it could be a reflection of lack of self-confidence or the social expectations regarding how they should behave. I can't say. In any case, I tried for a few years to be quiet and unobtrusive like them, but a certain tension developed until I had to say, "Hold on, something isn't working. This isn't me. I was brought up in the West, have a college education and have worked in the world, unlike the majority of the Tibetan nuns. It doesn't make sense for me to act like them; I have to act according to my culture." Coming to terms with this was a major turning point. I came to understand that spirituality is a process of inner transformation; it's not about squeezing myself into an artificial image of a good nun. It is okay to have an outgoing and straight-forward personality, but I need to transform my motivations and internal attitudes.

In 1986, I went to Taiwan to take bhikshuni vows, and stayed in Chinese monasteries for two months, which was a wonderful experience. Again, I was faced with the question, "What is Buddhism and what is culture?" I had "grown up" as a Buddhist in the Tibetan culture, and suddenly I was in a Chinese monastery, wearing Chinese robes, which are very different from the Tibetan ones I was accustomed to. Chinese culture is formal and things are done in a precise way, while Tibetan culture is much more relaxed. The Chinese nuns continuously had to fix my collar and adjust how I held my hands in prayer. In Tibetan monasteries we sit down during communal prayers, while in the Chinese monasteries, we stand up. My legs swelled because I wasn't used to standing hour after hour; I was used to sitting hour after hour! There were many changes like that: instead of prayers in Tibetan, they were in Chinese. The way of bowing was different, the etiquette was different.

This forced me to ask, "What is Buddhism?" It made me also acknowledge that I am not a Tibetan although I have spent years in that tradition; I'm not Chinese although I spent time there too. I am a Westerner and have to bring the essence of this religion into my own cultural context. That's a huge challenge, and we have to proceed slowly and carefully. If we discard everything we don't feel comfortable with, there's the danger of throwing the baby out with the bath water, of discarding or distorting the essence of the precious teachings in our attempt to free it from cultural forms which aren't our own. We are challenged to go beyond superficial discriminations to deep examination of what is spiritual practice.

It has become clear to me that spirituality isn't the clothes, the prayers, the monastery, the form. Real spirituality has to do with our own heart, our own mind, how we relate to people and how we relate to ourselves. It doesn't have color, shape or form, because our consciousness is without form, and this is what practice transforms. Nevertheless, since we live in society, we will evolve ways of sharing our internal understanding with others in ways fitting to our culture.

Western culture will influence Buddhism as it's practiced here. For example, in the West democracy is valued, while in Asia society is more hierarchical. If one is old, one's opinion is listened to; if one isn't, one's opinion doesn't have much weight. In fact, it would be considered inappropriate to challenge the elders' authority and wisdom. In the West, we are encouraged to express our opinions and we run organizations on a more democratic basis. As Buddhism comes to the West, I believe many of the hierarchical ways of thinking and acting will be left behind. On the other hand, anarchy isn't beneficial; we certainly need leaders, we need guidance from those with more wisdom than us. The Buddha set up the sangha community on a democratic basis with the monastics meeting and making decisions together. Yet, those who participated in the decision making were those with experience, not those who were new to the practice and lacked clarity about the path. Hopefully, our way of working together in Western Buddhist organizations can be similar to the Buddha's original intention.

In addition, the movement towards gender equality will influence Buddhism in the West. For example, in general the Tibetan nuns don't get the same education as the monks. Due to His Holiness the Dalai Lama's influence, this has begun to change in recent years, but it's still not equal. On the other hand, Western nuns and monks study in the same classes together, and my teachers give both nuns and monks positions of responsibility in Dharma centers. Women will be leaders in the Western Buddhist community. They will receive the same education as the men, and hopefully, the same respect and support. Although gender bias still exists in the West, we have the opportunity to establish new Buddhist institutions here that are more appreciative of women. In Asia, this will take longer because people's values are different and reforming existing institutions is sometimes more difficult than creating new ones.

Western Buddhism will also be influenced by social activism. During the Buddha's time, monastics were not encouraged to become involved in social issues or social welfare projects. Instead, they were to study, meditate, and by gaining realizations of the path, help society. But our social structure is different now as are the problems facing us. In ancient India, if one had a turn for the worse, the family would help out. One wouldn't wind up in the streets. Nor was there nuclear threat or danger from environmental pollution. Also, due to the Christian influence here, people expect monastics to be involved in charitable work. Therefore, His Holiness the Dalai Lama encourages us to learn from the Christians and to offer direct benefit to the society. This doesn't mean that all Buddhist monastics should run hospitals and schools. Rather, if it is suitable for one's practice and personality, one has the freedom to do that.

In the West, the relationship between monastics and lay followers will change. Western lay people aren't content simply to offer support and services so that the monastics can practice. They want to study and meditate as well. This is excellent. However, I hope that they will continue to support monastics, not because monastics are an elite, but because it helps everyone when some people devote their entire lives to study and practice. If we can help some people practice more diligently, then by gaining experience in the path, they'll be able to guide and teach us better.

The subject of Buddhist monasticism and Buddhism in the West is large, and this is simply a little taste. I hope it has been helpful.

Questions And Answers

Q. Sister Donald, could you speak about the relationship of the intellect and Christianity?

Sister Donald: This is a very important question that we could discuss for a long time. In *The Interior Castle*, Theresa of Avila said, "I came to the realization that the *mens* is not the *intellectus:* the superficial mind is not the intellect." It is significant that medieval persons understood that the superficial mind is not the deep mind. Medieval Christianity had a very deep regard for the way of the mind, in Buddhist terms you could call it the path of *jnana* or wisdom. Unfortunately, because of the scientific revolution of the seventeenth century and the enlightenment in the eighteenth century, Christianity backed away from those cultural currents and became primarily a way of *bakti*, a way of faith or of emotion. I think we need to recover the path of contemplative insight or knowledge. However, the problem is that much of contemporary theology is on the level of *mens* rather than *intellectus*. Sometimes it's even on the level of rational academic games, rather than deep contemplative insight which nourishes the *intellectus* as a spiritual faculty. We in the West no longer realize that the deep mind is a spiritual faculty. In fact, in academic and other circles, we make fun of the *intellectus* to some extent. We think that religion is separate from that. Thus, I believe that the path of knowledge needs to be recovered. There has been a fissure between intellect and emotion, intellect and faith, and we need a lot of work to turn that around.

Q. Both Christianity and Buddhism are male-centered, patriarchal religions. How can women find fulfillment in them?

Sister Donald: It's true; Christianity, and particularly Roman Catholicism, is male dominated. However, women have found meaning. We've come a long way in a short time, but we have a long way to go. If we look at particular issues, for example, the ordination of women, I think tremendous strides have been made in twenty years. However, there is still a long way to go to change the mentality of ordinary Christians, much less that of the hierarchy. Still, things are changing.

However, this is not simply about the internal struggles of women in the Church, but about how Western culture regards the feminine. We are discussing not only women's issues and the equality of the sexes, but the re-honoring of everything that Jung meant by the anima. We need to restore that part of our soul. The West has become, to some extent, soulless because of disparaging the feminine. This brought also the ecological rape of the Earth; everything follows from that. It's a much deeper issue than just internal struggles in our particular traditions. The evolution of consciousness is going on, and I have hope. Of course, there are some certain radical feminists who are much stronger about it than I am, and maybe they are therefore prophetic.

Ven. Chodron: Although historically there have been disparities between the power of men and women in Buddhist institutions, the institution isn't the practice. Spiritual practice goes beyond societal roles or stereotypes of male and female. It goes beyond the cultural discriminations reflected in institutions. Real practice happens in our hearts. As long as we are inspired to practice and have access to the teachings and the guidance of qualified teachers, then women can find fulfillment in a spiritual path. Religion is not the same as religious institutions. The latter were created by people, but the real essence of what we are trying to develop goes beyond institutions and whatever hierarchy and biases they may have.

Q. Can you say more about the intense pressure and heart required to let the luminosity shine within us?

Sister Donald: To the extent that I have studied spiritual traditions, the great spiritual literature, and the biographies of holy people, it is evident that transformation does not come without the intense pressure of our own work on ourselves, our own inner work, the inner alchemy that takes place in that crucible inside of us. The Old Testament says, "God is the Potter shaping the clay." Our life, the challenges and limitations we have, the blessings we have, everything is the hand of the Divine Potter shaping us. That is the intense pressure and intense heat that transform us into diamond. To the extent that we are awake and see that, to the extent that we cooperate with it and are open and are willing to be transformed, transformation happens.

Ven. Chodron: There's a lot of intense pressure and heat in Buddhist practice. Nowadays, some Westerners have the notion that spiritual practice is joy and bliss, love and light. Personally, I find it's learning to sit in a garbage dump with acceptance and inspiration. I can't speak for anyone else, but much of what goes on in my mind every day--the anger, jealousy, pride, grudges, attachment, competition--is garbage. I can't ignore that and live in a self-created realm of light and love. I have to deal with my garbage without identifying with it. That requires aspiration and energy, as well as gentle yet firm patience to continue on the path. Many people want instant enlightenment: Whammo! All my problems are gone! Unfortunately, it doesn't happen like that. Sister Donald, from what you say, it doesn't seem to happen like that according to your tradition either.

Sister Donald: One of the favorite quotations in the monasteries was, *"In patientia possidebitas animas vestras,"* "In patience you will possess your soul." *Patientia* means suffering.

Ven. Chodron: Many people would like fast food enlightenment. We want spirituality to be quick, cheap and easy; we'd like someone else to do the work for us. But this isn't possible. On one hand, we must accept ourselves, accept the garbage without getting depressed. Acceptance means we stop feeling guilty and being angry at ourselves because the internal garbage is there. It doesn't mean we just let those disturbing attitudes be. We must still exert constant energy and have a joyful aspiration to cleanse our minds and hearts and develop our qualities and potentials.

Q. Ven. Chodron, most Westerners have been brought up with the concept of a creator God. How did you balance your early upbringing with your later beliefs as a Tibetan Buddhist?

Ven. Chodron: In sharing my thoughts on this, I am not criticizing people who have different beliefs. I am only stating my own personal experience. When I was a teenager, long before I had contact with Buddhism, I attended Sunday School and learned about God, but I had difficulty understanding what was meant by God. I couldn't relate to the wrathful God of the

Old Testament, and couldn't understand the more loving God of the New Testament. I wondered, "If there is a God, how come things happen the way they do? Why does suffering continue to exist?" I didn't feel comfortable with the concepts of God that I had been introduced to. By the time I went to university, I had stopped believing in God, although I didn't know what I believed in.

Buddhism discussed rebirth, cause and effect (karma and its results), interdependence, and the lack of inherent existence. I was encouraged to think deeply about these to determine whether or not they explained my life and what I observed. As I did this, these ideas resonated in me. Because there was many years space between when I believed in God and when I accepted Buddhist explanations, I didn't encounter internal conflict in changing religions.

Sister Donald: As a Christian, I believe in a creator God and in creation. It's certainly part of the Creed. My experience of God is personal, particularly in the person of Jesus Christ, who St. Paul says is the icon of the invisible God. To me that's one of the best definitions of Christ: he is the icon of the invisible God. He is that door opened out onto the mystery. The mystery is so great that it cannot be circumscribed by any theology or any symbol. I have also gotten an insight into that mystery through Plotinius's concept of the one, which is the source; Plato's concept of the good; the Hindu concept of *satcitananda*. All of these reflect that deep, bottomless abyss of mystery which I know is creator God. All of these prisms can reflect that light.

Q. Please talk about the idea in Christianity of God being a personal God and your opinion of this.

Sister Donald: It is certainly part of the Judeo-Christian experience that we experience God as personal, as a being with whom we interact. God is not just a timeless absolute out there, a distant figure, or a deistic God who created the clock and got it running. God is personal, providential and loving, and we even have a human incarnate form in the person of Jesus Christ. Therefore, the experience of God is personal, and yet it's a person which opens out onto mystery.

Ven. Chodron: Buddhism, on the other hand, has no concept of a personal God or creator. There is belief in beings who are highly developed spiritually--the fully enlightened Buddhas, the liberated arhants--but these beings exist in the continuum from our present state. There are many Buddhas, not just Shakyamuni, who is the Buddha of this historical era. Those who are now Buddhas haven't always been Buddhas. They were once like us, confused, easily overcome by anger, clinging or ignorance. By practicing the path to purify these disturbing attitudes and to develop their good qualities, they transformed themselves. Thus the path is a matter of one's own internal growth. In Buddhism, there is no unbridgable gap between the holy beings and us. We too can purify our minds and develop our good qualities infinitely. We too can become fully enlightened beings, we have that Buddha potential.

Sister Donald: Although Christians believe in creator God and creatures who are finite, we are all called, as St. Peter says, to be partakers of the divine nature. Therefore, deification or theosis is what human existence is meant to be. We are called to become part of the Divine, to be full participants in the Divine. We are called to become partakers.

Ven. Chodron to Sister Donald: How much of the process of becoming divine depends on one's own determination and practice and how much on influence or grace from a supreme being?

Sister Donald: That is not an easy question to answer. How much is our work and how much is God's work, nature, grace and other factors? So many theological battles have been fought over this. In general, we in the Roman Catholic tradition believe that our freedom is called upon to be part of that process. It is not predestined, and salvation is not automatic. Salvation has been accomplished in Christ's redemption, but we have to open our souls. Purification, asceticism, spiritual work, practice and so forth are all needed. However, there's obviously a spectrum of opinions about this subject in the Christian tradition. Even somebody like Augustine, who was a figure in the early Church, fought with the Pelagians over this. The Pelagians said we've got to work harder while Augustine emphasized grace. It's a long, complicated story.

Ven. Chodron: Within Buddhism, there are also a variety of perspectives on this topic. Some traditions emphasize complete self-reliance, others stress depending on an external guide such as Amitabha Buddha. Personally speaking, I think it's somewhere in between. The Buddhas can teach, guide and inspire us, but they can't directly change us. We have to transform our own attitudes and actions. There's the saying that you can lead a horse to water, but you can't make it drink. Spiritual transformation is similar. We aren't alone in an unfriendly universe; the Buddhas and bodhisattvas definitely help us by teaching, setting a good example and inspiring us. On the other hand, if they had the power to stop all our suffering, they

43

would have. But they can't; only we can transform our own minds. They teach us, but we have to put it into practice.

Q. How can a mother integrate the monastic life style into her life?

Sister Donald: Diedrich Bonnhoffer, the great Lutheran pastor and spiritual writer, said God must be met in the midst of life. That is the key. Whatever your vocation, or your responsibilities in life, that's your path. God must be met in the everyday ordinary obligations of life. The monastic impulse is characterized by living out of one's center, not living in dispersion. The mother of a family must find that inner center out of which to serve her family and to deal with the challenges and trials of household life. Just a week ago there was a review in the *New York Times* of a book by the sociologist Robert Bellah called *The Good Society.* Bellah believes that the answer to many of the problems of American society is what he calls "attention"--not allowing our lives to be dissipated, but to live consciously and with attentiveness. In my eyes, that is living monastically in its widest sense. Transformation of society can't be accomplished without personal transformation according to Bellah. This is a profound truth, which is so important in our time.

Ven. Chodron: I agree with you. It's the daily life practice that counts. We shouldn't think that religion, meditation and spirituality are over here, and work, family and daily life are over there. The two are joined. To make them come together, it's important to keep some quiet time every day to be alone, to get centered, to reflect on our motivations and actions, and to make some resolutions. This prevents us from living in dispersion. Every morning or evening, we can take fifteen minutes or a half hour and sit, breathe, look at our lives, cultivate loving-kindness. If we do this in the morning, then in the evening we can look back at what we felt and did during the day and see what went well and what needs to be improved. This isn't evaluation of external events, but our attitudes and actions. Did we get angry? How can we avoid that in similar situations in the future? Were we understanding of someone who criticized us? How can we increase that patience? By using the quiet time to look at our life and mind and to cultivate kind attitudes, we can carry those attitudes into our daily lives. Becoming holy doesn't mean looking holy, it means feeling kind, being wise and living from this center.

Q. Please speak about the value of a monastic way of life.

Ven. Chodron: Sister Donald, people ask me and they probably ask you too, "Aren't you escaping from reality by being a nun?" They must think it's easy to escape from our problems; all one has to do is change clothes and move to a different building! If it were that easy, I think everybody would become monks and nuns! However, the problem is our anger, our attachment, our ignorance, and they come with us wherever we go, inside a monastery or out. In fact, when we live in a monastery, we see our disturbing attitudes more clearly. In lay life, we can go home, close the door and do what we want. When we live in a monastery, we live with people who may not be the kind of people we would choose as friends. But we have to learn to care for them, not superficially, but deeply. We can't close the door and do our own thing. The monastic way of life brings us in touch with where we're at. There's no escaping.

Sister Donald: I was reading a wonderful interview with the Dalai Lama this morning in which he talked about the joys of living in community and the luxury of monastic life. Our life and our time are free to engage in spiritual practice. He remarked, "In the life of a married householder one gives up half of one's freedom right away." I paused to think about that and concluded, "In monastic life we give up *all* our freedom right away."

Q. Ven. Chodron, please explain rebirth.

Ven. Chodron: Rebirth is based on there being a continuity of mind. Mind or consciousness doesn't refer to the brain, which is the physical organ, or just to the intellect. It's the aware and experiential part of us that perceives, feels, thinks and cognizes. Our mind is a continuum, one moment of mind following the next. When we're alive, our gross consciousness operates: we see, hear, taste, smell, touch and think. But when we die, our body loses the ability to support consciousness, and during the death process, our mind gradually dissolves into a very subtle state and eventually leaves the body at the moment of death. Influenced by our previous actions, our mind transmigrates to another body.

Some people ask, "If there's a mind that transmigrates from one body to another, then isn't that a soul?" From a Buddhist viewpoint, no. Soul implies a solid, fixed personality, something that is me. But in Buddhism, the mind is a flux, it's a continuum that's changing moment by moment. For example, when we superficially look at the Mississippi River, we say, " There's the Mississippi River. " But if, through analysis, we were to try to find the Mississippi River, to isolate something that is it, could we find it? Is the Mississippi River the water? the banks? the silt? Is it the river in Missouri or the one

46

in Louisiana? We can't find anything solid or permanent to isolate as the river because the river is made of parts and it's constantly changing.

Our mindstream is similar. It changes each moment. We don't think or feel the same in any two moments. When we analyze, we can't isolate anything as the mind or as me. There's nothing to identify as a solid personality or soul. But when we don't analyze and just speak superficially, we can say, "I'm walking" or "I'm thinking." This is said on the basis of there being a continuum of moments of mind or body that are constantly changing, the later ones depending on the former ones. There is no fixed soul or personality that goes from life to life.

Sister Donald: Surely many people are wondering what I think about reincarnation. If there is rebirth, I want at least two weeks off in between! The Roman Catholic tradition has taken a strong stand against reincarnation. I can accept that, but also I have no strong reason for opposing or affirming the idea of rebirth. I am open, and have bracketed the question. I do see a deep resemblance between the Buddhist teaching and Catholic teaching on the process of the spiritual path: both say we need ongoing purification, education and formation. Roman Catholicism talks about purgatory. That is, when people die, they are not necessarily ready to see the face of God and need further transformation. Here we find some similarity with reincarnation: the basic theme is that we do need much education, formation and purification to be able to see God. This makes perfect sense to me. There is, I think, a deep kind of harmony between Buddhism and Catholicism here.

Q. Why do some Christian groups consider various Eastern meditation practices as cults or as being influenced by the devil?

Sister Donald: I know that they do, but not why they do. The wider ecumenical view goes back to the early struggle within Christianity to break out of the Jewish, into the Hellenistic and pagan world of the time. Breaking out into the Greek philosophical categories of thought was a struggle. Even as early as the second century, we find the Christian theologian and apologist, Justin Martyr, who said, "Wherever you find truth, there you find Christ." Why some Christians don't have that point of view I couldn't say exactly, except that I think it is mistaken and relies on a very narrow meaning of Scripture. But the Catholic tradition has solidly had that large ecumenical point of view almost right from the beginning. For example, the first one to translate the Koran in medieval Europe was Peter the Venerable, a Benedictine Abbot.

Ven. Chodron: In Buddhism, we say that if a certain belief or practice helps one to become a better person, then practice it. It doesn't matter who said it. For example, both Jesus and the Buddha spoke on loving-kindness and compassion, on patience and non-violence. Because these qualities lead us to temporal and ultimate happiness, we should put the teachings on them into practice, regardless of who taught them.

Q. Please describe your daily practice or prayer and meditation. What is it like to meditate in your tradition?

Sister Donald: Our whole prayer life as Benedictines is in the setting, the culture if you will, of the liturgy. We recite the Divine Office together four or five times a day. Continual saturation with scripture "seeds" the deepest place in us. We are taught to do spiritual reading prayerfully and contemplatively, especially reading of Scripture, early Church writers (Fathers

48

of the Church) and great monastic authors. There is very little method in the Benedictine way. In the past two decades there has been more taking up of specific methods such as centering prayer (which is actually an ancient way). Meditation is deliberate introversion. In our day and age there is a greater need for Christian monastics to be consciously committed meditators with a specific practice. All of our life forms us and cultivates our soul; but deliberate, apophatic, non-image meditation can be very helpful. Also, there is so much wisdom and living spiritual transmission in the hesychast (Jesus Prayer) tradition. But again, it is not just a technique; it is a whole way of life. Increasing "conversion" leads to deeper and deeper kenosis or self-emptying. As we are transformed more and more it spills over into *diakonia* (service) and *koinonia* (community).

Ven. Chodron: Here I'll speak about my personal practice, but each person practices differently. There are certain meditations and prayers that I've promised to do every day. When I wake up in the morning, I do some of these for an hour and a half or two hours. The rest I do later in the day. This adds stability to my life, for the first thing every morning is quiet time for reflection. A nun's life can be very busy--teaching, counseling, writing, organizing--so having time for meditation in the morning and later in the day is very important. Sometimes, I do retreat, which involves meditating eight to ten hours a day and living in silence. Retreat is nurturing because it provides the opportunity to go deeper into the practice, for the purpose of being able to benefit all beings more effectively through first improving oneself.

In Buddhism, there are two basic forms of meditation. One is to develop mental stability or concentration, the other to gain insight or understanding through investigation. I do both of these. My practice also includes visualization and mantra recitation.

Q. Please comment on the relationship of religion and psychology. Is there a difference between spiritual and psychological growth? Can one be highly evolved spiritually and still have psychological problems?

Sister Donald: Certainly, but true growth in the Spirit should bring healing on deeper and deeper levels. However, even a schizophrenic *may* be a saint. We cannot bypass the psychological to get to the spiritual. It is a very complex question, and I wish we had more time to deal with it.

Ven. Chodron: Religion and psychology have similarities as well as differences. Psychology is directed more towards mental health and happiness in the present life, while religion looks further and seeks not only present fortune, but transcendence of the limited human situation. In fact, to transcend our limitations, we have to be willing to give up the attachment to present happiness.

To have genuine spiritual growth, one must have corresponding psychological growth. In my view, people who have mystical experiences and then get angry because the toast is burnt have missed the boat. Transcendence isn't about having temporary peak experiences, it's about deep, long-lasting transformation. It involves freeing ourselves from anger, attachment, jealousy and pride. This is a slow and gradual process, and people can be at various points along the continuum to enlightenment.

The Value Of A Monastic Way Of Life

by His Holiness the Dalai Lama

Although I have had the opportunity and privilege to participate in many interfaith dialogues and interfaith services, this current dialogue has had a totally different significance. I am particularly curious to know the opinion of my fellow Buddhist monks here about the fact that I have read and commented on the Christian gospel.

You know, obviously, personally, I am a Buddhist. Therefore, my own faith does not include the belief in a "Creator." But at the same time, I really want to help those who say they are Christian practitioners to strengthen their faith and their sincere practice. I really try to help them.

There is a story: once Nagarjuna wanted to debate with a great scholar, a non-Buddhist in the ancient Indian tradition. His disciple, Aryadeva, offered to go in his place so that his teacher need not go. Nagarjuna said, "First I must test you to see if you are qualified to take my place." Nagarjuna and Aryadeva began to debate, with Nagarjuna taking the position of the ancient Indian school against which Aryadeva would debate. Nagarjuna's defense of the non-Buddhist school of thought was so convincing and firm that there was a point in the debate that Aryadeva began to doubt his teacher's allegiance.

This might apply similarly to a Buddhist monk who tries to understand about the "Creator." (laughter) These few days of dialogue and discussions have reinforced my longheld belief that in spite of the fundamental metaphysical and philosophical differences in the religious traditions of the world, there is enough strong, common ground that unites the various religious traditions, thus enabling us to make a common contribution towards the betterment of humanity. My experience over the last few days has strengthened this belief, so I feel very grateful for the opportunity to have led this year's John Main Seminar.

Here today in this monastery I would like to speak on the value of the monastic way of life. The monastic life is the way of life based on explicitly following certain precepts and vows. I will discuss how that could be a foundation for one's spiritual practice and growth.

Although my fellow Buddhist monks here are familiar with this idea, let me say that in the Buddhist tradition, when we speak of our spiritual path or enlightenment, the practice is explained within the framework of what are known as the three higher trainings. These are the higher training in wisdom, the higher training in concentration or meditation, and the higher training in morality. Of these three, the higher training in morality and ethics is the foundation on which the remaining two trainings are based.

It is in the context of the higher training in morality that we speak about our moral precepts and ethical disciplines. Generally speaking, in the Buddhist tradition there are two types of precepts: the lay person's ethical precepts and the monastic precepts. In Buddhism the area of ethical discipline is known as *pratimoksha*, which literally means "individual liberation." In that practice there are primarily seven or eight sets of precepts, of which five are monastic. They include novitiate vows up to the full ordination for men and women. The two remaining sets of precepts are those of the lay practitioners.

When speaking about monastic precepts, we are referring to an ethically disciplined way of life based on the foundational precept of celibacy. To reflect on the importance and value of a monastic way of life, it is important to understand the wider religious and spiritual context within which such a way of life is adopted. For example, in the case of Buddhism, there is the belief that every living being possesses the potential for perfection, the Buddha nature, and this is inherent in all of us. This seed of Buddhahood is naturally present in each being. In the language of Christianity, used by my brother and sister Christian practitioners, the expression is slightly different. One says that all human beings share the divine nature, God's "image and likeness." Thus in both religions, there is the idea of a natural purity in all of us which is the foundation for our spiritual growth. To perfect that nature of goodness in all of us, it is not sufficient to enhance and develop it. At the same time we also need to decrease and overcome the negative impulses and tendencies that are within us. We need a two-pronged approach: enhancing the positive qualities and decreasing the negative impulses.

I believe that one of the principal ideas underlying the monastic way of life is the idea of contentment. This principle of contentment is associated with simplicity and modesty. The emphasis on and practice of simplicity and modesty are common to both the Christian and the Buddhist monastic orders. For example, in the case of Buddhism, this is found in the list of twelve qualities to be cultivated by a member of the monastic order and the four tendencies of a superior being. (These have to do with being content with simple food, clothing, shelter, and having a strong interest in pacifying the mental defilements and practicing meditation to generate excellent qualities.) These instructions enable the individual practitioner to live a way of life in which he or she is content with modest needs in terms of food, shelter, clothing, and so on. This helps that person develop not only a sense of contentment, but also a strength of character so that he or she does not become soft and weak and succumb to temptations for a luxurious way of life.

The stronger the character that you have, the stronger your will and your capacity to endure hardship. With these you will have greater power of enthusiasm and perseverance. Once you have that kind of powerful enthusiasm and sense of endurance and forbearance, they will lay a firm foundation for further spiritual progress such as attaining single-pointedness of mind and penetrating insight.

In the case of my brother and sister Christian practitioners, especially those in the monastic order, I think you need more intense effort and perseverance because you will have only one life; whereas the Buddhist monastic members can be a little lazy because if they do not make it in this life, there is another life! (laughter)

One of the principal benefits of having such a strong force of endurance and forbearance is that it lays the foundation for future spiritual development. For example, if you look at the list of conditions that are recommended for someone who is aspiring to attain tranquil abiding, or *shamatha*, we find that some of the principal conditions recommended are a sense of contentment and modesty and an ethically sound and disciplined way of life.

A monastic way of life is a life of self-discipline. It is important that we do not think of this discipline as being imposed from outside upon us by an irresistible power. Discipline must come from within. It should be based on clear awareness of its value as well as a certain degree of introspection and mindfulness. Once you have such an attitude towards discipline, it will be self-adopted rather than imposed. Being freely chosen, discipline will really help you develop two very important qualities of the mind: alertness and mindfulness. As you develop these two basic factors of awakening, you will have the most powerful tools to attain single-pointedness of the mind.

When we examine the value of the Buddhist monastic order, it is important to see that celibacy is the foundation. We must understand why celibacy has to be the foundation of a monastic way of life. In one sense, the way of life of a celibate monastic almost resembles going against the biological nature of our body. If you look at the nature of sexuality and sexual desire, it is very much part of our biological impulses. This drive is associated with the evolutionary process of reproduction. In some sense, yes, a monastic way of life is against the biological nature of the body.

What is the goal or purpose of adopting such a way of life? For a Buddhist practitioner, and particularly for a Buddhist monk or nun, the ultimate goal is the attainment of nirvana or liberation. This is liberation of the mind. If you understand nirvana and liberation properly, you know that by seeking liberation we are trying to go beyond the bonds of human nature, to transcend the limitations of human existence. Since the goal is beyond the bounds of human existence, then, of course, the method to be adopted will also involve going against biological limitations. The celibate way of life acts as perhaps the most powerful antidote to overcome the impulses and acts of attachment and clinging desire. According to Buddhism, attachment and clinging desire lie at the root of our cyclic existence. Since the goal is to cut the knot of that cycle and go beyond it, the means will also involve going against the currents of the biological nature.

The Buddhist presentation of the evolution of samsara is depicted in the form of a cycle, the twelve links of interdependent origination, which clearly demonstrate how attachment and clinging act as the roots of cyclic existence. For example, a person may have fundamental ignorance, the first link, and may have created karma, the second link, and may have experienced the third link, consciousness, where the karmic seed has been implanted. However, if that karmic seed is not activated by clinging desire and attachment, samsaric rebirth cannot come into being. This shows how desire and attachment lie at the root of our cyclic existence.

In the Christian context I offer my own personal opinion and understanding, and my friend here, Father Laurence, may have a more profound account to give. But in any case, I will try to look at the role and importance of celibacy in the Christian monastic context. Since there is no idea of nirvana as the Buddhist presents it, I think celibacy has to be understood in relation to the fundamental, important principle of being modest and contented. This is understood in relation to fulfilling one's call or destiny, allowing oneself the time and opportunity for spiritual practice, and committing and dedicating oneself completely to one's calling.

It is important to lead a modest way of life so that there are no personal involvements and obligations which would divert one's attention from the pursuit of that calling. This is essential. If you compare a monastic's life with a family life, the latter clearly has greater involvements. One has more obligations and responsibilities in a family life. In contrast, at least ideally, a monk or nun's life reflects the ideal of simplicity and freedom from obligations. Our principle should be this: as far as our own interests and needs in life are concerned, there should be as little obligation and as little involvement as possible; but insofar as others' interests are concerned, the monks and nuns should have as much involvement as possible and as many commitments as possible.

I was told that in the Benedictine monastic order there are three precepts which are emphasized. These are: first, the vow of obedience; second, the "conversion of life," implying that there ought to be an ever-growing evolution within one's spiritual life; and third, the precept of stability. Let me again look at these three vows, wearing Buddhist spectacles. I think the first vow, the vow of obedience, has a close parallel to the Buddhist monks' and nuns' obedience to the *Pratimoksha Sutra*, which is the Buddhist scripture laying down the rules and precepts for a monastic way of life. This sutra in the Buddhist tradition has to be recited every fortnight during the confession ceremonies. In some sense, this recitation affirms our obedience to the Buddha's monastic precepts. Just as the members of the monastic order reaffirm their obedience to the scriptures every fortnight (and this is often expressed by living in accord with certain rules of obedience within the monastic community itself), the internal discipline of the monastery is supposed to reflect the spirit and the precepts set down by the Buddha.

This two-fold obedience, I think, is similar to that of the Christian practice. Not only does one have the personal monastic precepts, but there is also a vow of obedience to the discipline of the monastery. By obeying the internal discipline of the monastery and the dictates of the abbot and the senior members of the monastery, you are in fact paying homage and obedience to the precepts and rules set down by the Buddha himself. This is very similar to the idea found in the Gospel when Jesus says, "Those who listen to me, do not listen to me but listen to Him, the Father who sent me."

The second precept of the Benedictine order, conversion of life, is really the key to the monastic life. It emphasizes the importance of bringing about inner spiritual transformation.

Even if someone leads a totally secluded life with no contact whatsoever with the outside world, if no internal transformation takes place, then the life is pretty useless. In Tibet we have an expression that sums up the urgency and importance of this conversion of life in the monastic order. One Tibetan master said, "If I have a month or two more to live, I will be able to prepare for my next life. If I have a year or more to live, I will be able to take care of my ultimate aspiration." This demonstrates the urgency on the part of the practitioner to work constantly on bringing about internal transformation. A process of growth must take place within the practitioner.

I think stability, the third vow, points toward the importance of maintaining a stable way of life, not only physically but also mentally. In that way one's mind is not infected by all sorts of curiosities, distractions and so on.

When I look at these three vows, I personally see the middle one as being the most important: the conversion of life, which is the need to have ever-increasing spiritual growth within oneself. To help create the right condition for that you need the first vow, which is the vow of obedience. The third vow enables the person to overcome obstacles along the way, to protect himself or herself from being affected by hindrances. The first vow creates the favorable conditions, the third helps you to overcome the obstacles and hindrances, but the second is the main vow.

Having said all this, I do not mean to imply that even in the Buddhist context there is no hope for liberation or nirvana without joining the monastic order. That is not the case. For someone who can embark upon a spiritual path, attainment of nirvana can even be possible while maintaining the life of a householder. Similarly, one might join the monastic order and lead a secluded life, but if there is no internal transformation, there is no nirvana or liberation for that person. It is for this reason that when the Buddha gave teachings on morality he spoke about not only monastic precepts but also precepts for lay persons. I think this is also true in the case of Christianity; all human beings equally share the divine nature so all of us have the potential to perfect that and thus experience union with the divine being. With that, my brief presentation is over. If I have made any false interpretations, I would like to apologize. (laughter)

Father Laurence Freeman: Your Holiness, the early Christian monks came from the Egyptian desert. Disciples or seekers of the truth would go to the desert to seek out the wisest teacher, and they would simply say, "Father, give us a word." We asked you to do that for us today, and you have given us a very rich and wise word. Thank you.

His Holiness suggests that we take five minutes of silence together now.

Love Unbounded

by Sister Candasiri

Some years ago Sister Rosemary from the Order of the Sisters of the Love of God came to spend two months at Amaravati Buddhist Monastery to pursue her interest in meditation, stimulated through reading the teachings of our abbot, Ajahn Sumedho. After discovering, in addition to a deep sense of spiritual friendship, that we had been at school together almost thirty years before, we kept in contact. I was delighted when an opportunity came to pay her a visit.

From the moment Sister Medhanandi, who is also a nun from Amaravati Monastery, and I stepped off the bus in Oxford and were met by Sister Rosemary, we were made to feel at ease. As three brown-robed figures conversing animatedly as we walked through the streets, we attracted a certain interest: her elaborate head dress and gold crucifix, our shaven heads, and all of us wearing sandals. We made our way to the convent which is situated on a quiet suburban road. It consists of several buildings constructed over a time span of about one hundred years and is set in five acres of enclosed gardens where fruit and vegetables are grown and formal gardens merge with less cultivated areas.

As we entered the cool silence of the enclosure our voices naturally dropped to a whisper and then to silence in accordance with the rule followed by the community. This simple observance brings an aura of quiet collectedness as the sisters move about in the cloisters. Most communication happens by notes--each sister has a note clip in the main hallway--or by gesture. When meeting the superior, Mother Anne, I noticed we all felt a slight awkwardness in finding suitable gestures of respect and greeting, but we knew we were welcome.

It was our intention to merge as much as possible into the daily life of the community. However, Sister Rosemary, although appreciative of our intention to be as discreet a presence as possible, had other ideas. I was surprised to see on the daily schedule thoughtfully prepared for us in our cells "morning puja" and "evening puja," as well as group discussion and meditation workshop on Saturday afternoon. These were to take place in the Chapter House, which had been set aside for us to use during our stay. We attended their Offices in the chapel, including the Night Office from 2 to 3 am, and helped with simple domestic duties--washing up, sewing curtains and taking care of the refectory. At suitable times and in suitable places we also did a fair bit of talking. So our days were well-filled, and yet somehow there was a sense of spaciousness. Each moment felt precious as we drank from the well of goodness that we found there.

As we entered the chapel it was natural to bow--a deep bow from the waist--and we were seated among the professed sisters. For some of them it must have felt very strange to have us there and included to such a degree. For our part, we felt deeply touched. I looked at the faces of the sisters sitting opposite to us, many of them getting older now, some of them very old. From some one could sense the struggle of the life, from others there seemed to emanate a radiance--the beauty of one who is whole and at peace with existence. For each I felt deep respect and gratitude.

We ate with the community and the other female and male guests at long wooden tables in the refectory. The midday meal, which was eaten from a single wooden bowl, was accompanied each day by a reading on aspects of spiritual life. During our stay the theme was celibacy in religious commuity and the integration of the active and contemplative aspects of our life. It seemed strikingly pertinent.

The sisters, concerned that it might not interest us, were somewhat hesitant about inviting us to their choir practice. Each week an elderly monk from another Order nearby visits "to try to teach us to sing," as one of the sisters explained. But it was a delight to experience their interaction with him and to hear their Eastertide Alleluias soar to the highest heavens. One felt they were simply brother and sisters in the holy life. In contrast, we noticed at the communion service we attended the first morning of our visit the immediate sense of polarity which arose with the entry of the priest. Until that time we had all simply been religious people; suddenly in relation to him, we became "women."

Each morning and evening we met in the Chapter House with those of the community who wished to attend our puja and meditation. Although the sisters do not receive training in formal meditation, as we sat together the quality of silence and still attention was quite remarkable. One sensed that this presence of mind was the result of years of silent prayerfulness and recitation of the Office--an austere and impressive practice.

Our discussions were lively. Although they keep silence for much of the time, the recreation periods two or three times a week encourage discussion and stimulate a keen interest and reflection on many aspects of life. They were very interested in the Buddhist approach to working with the mind. It was a revelation to them that significant changes in the mind and mental states could be effected simply through patiently bearing with them; there was no need to struggle or to feel guilty or burdened by the negativity, doubt or confusion that affect us all. Also interesting to them were the practices of walking meditation and of just sitting consciously as ways of attuning to the physical body.

We talked together about many things, aware that what we shared was vastly greater than our differences. It was clear that we could learn from and support one another without compromising our commitment to our respective traditions in any way. It was also touching to realize that we experienced the same personal doubts and sense of inadequacy, and that each felt the other to be stronger or more impressive. I sensed the fragility and subtlety of the renunciant life, demanding as it does the surrender of personal power and control; the need to give of oneself totally and, as one sister put it, simply to "trust the process."

I met with Sister Helen Mary, who is eighty-four years old now. Having lived alone for twenty-five years on Bardsey Island, she has the appearance of one well worn by the elements of nature. Again I felt a shyness, a hesitation: should we bow, shake hands, or what? But that seemed to be a very minor matter! She spoke gently and quietly but with great enthusiasm about the wonder of living "immersed in the spirit." I knew what she meant, although I would have used different words.

On the last morning of our stay, we met with Mother Anne. I was curious to know how she regarded our visit and Sister Rosemary's great interest in the Buddhist tradition. She told us that she had had no doubts about receiving us and that she felt that nowadays it is essential to recognize God beyond the limitations of any particular religious convention. This was clearly conveyed when we finally took our leave, as she enveloped each of us in turn with the most whole-hearted embrace that I have ever experienced! There was no doubt about the "Love of God"--or whatever name one would like to call it--that we shared at that moment.

At the last Office, with the afternoon sunlight filtering through the lofty windows of the chapel, I was struck by the awesome purity of the life: its simplicity and renunciation, its total dedication to what is wholly good. Beside it, the outside world we were about to enter seemed overwhelmingly confused and complicated. There is so little in our society to encourage people to live carefully, so much to stimulate greed and selfishness. Later on I realized that many visitors experience our Buddhist monastic life in much the same way, even though from the inside it can often seem quite ordinary and full of flaws.

As we waited with Sister Rosemary for our bus back to London, we continued to talk about meditation and mindfulness. Meanwhile, the bus we were due to catch sailed by. Oh mindfulness! Not long after another came, and more attentive this time, we managed to make it stop for us. We parted, our hearts full and deeply grateful.

Biographies of the Contributors

In the order in which they appear in this book:

Sister Donald Corcoran

Sister Donald Corcoran, OSB, Cam., is a native of Minnesota, USA. She has been a Benedictine nun for thirty-five years. From 1976 to 1979, Sister Donald was co-director of the Institute of Religious Formation at St. Louis University where she also headed the M.A. in spirituality. She remains an adjunct professor at St. Louis University where she returns every January to teach a course on the history of Christian spirituality. She has a Ph.D. in theology from Fordham University with a specialization in spirituality. Her dissertation is entitled "The Spiritual Guide: Midwife of the Higher Spiritual Self," a study of the classic master/disciple relationship in the great spiritual traditions. In 1979, she helped found the Transfiguration Monastery in Windsor, New York, where she currently lives. Her present interest is a comparative study of Benedictine and Confucian spirituality.

Venerable Thubten Chodron

Born in 1950, Thubten Chodron (then Cherry Greene) graduated with a B.A. in History from the U.C.L.A. in 1971. After traveling in Europe, North Africa and Asia for one and a half years, she got a teaching credential and attended the University of Southern California to do post-graduate studies in Education while working as a teacher in the Los Angeles City School System. In 1975, she attended a meditation course given by

Ven. Lama Yeshe and Ven. Zopa Rinpoche, and subsequently went to their monastery in Nepal to continue to study and practice Buddha's teachings. In 1977, she received the sramanerika (novice) ordination, and in 1986, went to Taiwan to take the bhikshuni (full) ordination.

She studied and practiced Buddhism of the Tibetan tradition for many years in India and Nepal. She then directed the spiritual program at Lama Tzong Khapa Institute in Italy, and later studied at Dorje Pamo Monastery in France. She has taught Buddhist philosophy and meditation in Europe, Asia, North America, Eastern Europe and the former Soviet Union. She currently lives and teaches in Seattle with Dharma Friendship Foundation. Her books include *Open Heart, Clear Mind*; *What Color Is Your Mind?*; *Taming the Monkey Mind*, and *Glimpse of Reality* (with Dr. Alexander Berzin).

His Holiness the Fourteenth Dalai Lama

His Holiness the Fourteenth Dalai Lama, Tenzin Gyatso, is the spiritual and temporal leader of the Tibetan people. Born to a peasant family, he was recognized at the age of two as the reincarnation of the Thirteenth Dalai Lama. He completed the traditional monastic studies and was awarded the Geshe degree (Ph.D.) in Buddhist philosophy. Due to the political situation in Tibet and the threat of Chinese occupation, His Holiness was asked to assume leadership as head of state of his country when he was fifteen years old. After an abortive uprising against Chinese occupation of Tibet in 1959, His Holiness and tens of thousands of Tibetans were forced into exile. In India, they have established the Tibetan government-in-exile in Dharmsala, where His Holiness currently lives. He continues to teach Buddhism untiringly to all who wish to hear and integrates his spiritual practice with a life of service, leading the Tibetan people to preserve and adapt their culture in their exile communities as they await the return to their homeland. His Holiness travels extensively, speaking on such subjects as universal responsibility, love, kindness, and compassion, and his books have been published in a variety of Western languages. In 1989, His Holiness was awarded the Nobel Peace Prize.

Sister Candasiri

Sister Candasiri was born in England in 1947 and brought up as a practicing Christian. After graduating from university, she practiced meditation in several different traditions and in 1977, met Ajahn Sumedho, an American monk ordained in the Theravada tradition of Thailand. She was one of the first four women ordained at the newly established Chithurst Buddhist Monastery in West Sussex. Having taken the eight precept ordination (anagarika) in 1979, she took the ten precepts (siladhara) in 1983. Currently she lives at Chithurst Monastery where she is helping to establish a training program for nuns and female anagarikas. She also teaches meditation retreats in the U.K. and abroad.

Further Reading

Aitken, Robert and Steindl-Rost, David, *The Ground We Share*. Triumph Books; Liguori, Missouri, 1994.

Dharma, Karuna and Kerze, Michael, ed., *An Early Journey: The Los Angeles Buddhist-Roman Catholic Dialogue*. Los Angeles, 1991.

Indapanno, Bhikkhu Buddhadasa, *Christianity and Buddhism*. Bangkok.

Kamenetz, Rodger, *The Jew in the Lotus*. Harper Collins Publishers; New York, 1994.

Walker, Susan, ed., *Speaking of Silence*. Paulist Press; New York, 1987.

Yeshe, Lama, *Silent Mind, Holy Mind*. Wisdom Publication, Boston, 1995.

ACKNOWLEDGEMENT

This book is sponsored by Mr William Chua Geok Eng in memory of his late father, Mr Chua Kim Cheng, so that this book could be sold to its readers at a subsized rate. May he attain the supreme bliss of Nirvana.

DANA PROMOTION PTE LTD

Dana Promotion Pte. Ltd. was formed by a group of Buddhists with the objective of promoting Buddhist economy. It is the local distributor of a few Buddhist publications. Book mailing service is also available. Readers can acquire more details from:

Dana Promotion Pte. Ltd.,
c/o Block 31
Dover Road,
#05-117,
Singapore 130031,
Pager No: 9214 8469
Fax: (65) 5697185